Why I Believe in God

and Other Reflections by Children

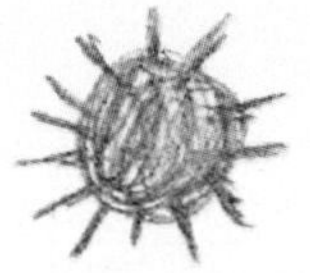

Dandi Daley Mackall

PRIMA PUBLISHING

Library of Congress Cataloging-in-Publication Data

Why I believe in God : and other reflections by children / [compiled by] Dandi Daley Mackall.

p. cm.

Summary: A collection of writings and artwork reflecting a cross-section of children's thoughts about God, as selected by the compiler from more than 4500 submissions.

ISBN 0-7615-1649-2

1. Children—Religious life. [1. God. 2. Children's writings. 3. Children's art.] I. Mackall, Dandi Daley.

BL625.5W54 1999

200'.83—dc21 99-37229

CIP

99 00 01 02 03 GG 10 9 8 7 6 5 4 3 2 1

Printed in the United States of America

HOW TO ORDER

Single copies may be ordered from Prima Publishing, P.O. Box 1260BK, Rocklin, CA 95677; telephone (916) 632-4400. Quantity discounts are also available. On your letterhead, include information concerning the intended use of the books and the number of books you wish to purchase.

Visit us online at www.primalifestyles.com

This book is dedicated to
every child I had the
privilege of talking with about
God—and to God who has
given all of you so much
wisdom and love.

Introduction

No wonder so many adults want to be children again! For over a year I traveled across the United States speaking in elementary schools and asking children about God, faith, and life. I received over 4,500 essays from children who believe in God with a matter-of-fact faith. God is as real to them as baseball and ice cream, as true as sunlight and Saturdays.

This book attempts to capture a cross-section of the wisdom and insight of children. As you read—and laugh—through this book, you'll learn everything from the fact that heaven doesn't have salad to the common-sense rationale that belief makes you better than you are now. Hopefully, some of the child-like faith revealed in these pages will rub off on us. And we can relax a little, knowing that these children will carry us into the next millennium with faith and hope.

I believe in God because He will not ever turn me down for someone better, prettier, or smarter.

Jessica Simpson

age 12

I love God the most because He's really strong and that means He will wash up my sins and clean up my messes.

Alex Smith
age 5

When I grow up, I think God wants me to be a missionary. But what I want to be is someone who works at the cash register. So maybe I'll try to be, like a missionary with a cash register.

Elizabeth Thompson
age 6

I believe in God, but I still wonder about a lot of things. Like I wonder how He made eyeballs.

Joseph Langer
age 7

There are so many people talking to God at the same time. He listens to every one of them and doesn't even have call waiting.

Cortni Smeltzer

age 11

God is pretty old, like about 25 years old, but he looks a lot younger.

Kelsi Wilson, age 6

I think God looks like a Hispanic-Chinese person because I think he's black and white so that kinda equals to Hispanic-Chinese.

-Rachel McKelvy-
age 9

The only people God made really big and growed was Adam and Eve and he had to make them grown ups because they had to name the animals.

Dustin Laumach

age 6

God is very powerful. He made the whole world in six days. It takes me that long to clean my room.

Sarah Roark

age 11

The funny thing
is we don't
Know if God is
a he or a she.
And So thats
Why they call
God thee.

Jeff Smith
age 7

When you die, if you get to go to heaven God brings you a ladder. If you don't get to go to heaven, the devil gives you a elevator going down.

Joey S. Giardina
age 7

God
Devil

I think God is there even when I don't want him there.

Sierra Wood
age 9

Everybody should spend more time with God. Don't just talk to him on business.

Zachery Russell
age 8

If you don't believe in God,
you haven't given him a
chance. Pray to him like
when you're scared, like
at the San Diego zoo on
the coaster ride.

Mychelle Clark
age 6

God is someone real and I try to make Him my idol. I can admit it is hard, because all these cute actors are coming out. But God seems like the only one I actually have a chance of meeting someday.

Katelyn Mooney
Age 11

Angels bring messages to North Africa, kentuckys and America. Some of the messages are happy and some are like "you might be dying soon" or "you're going to the loin's den."

Cody Braden
Age 6

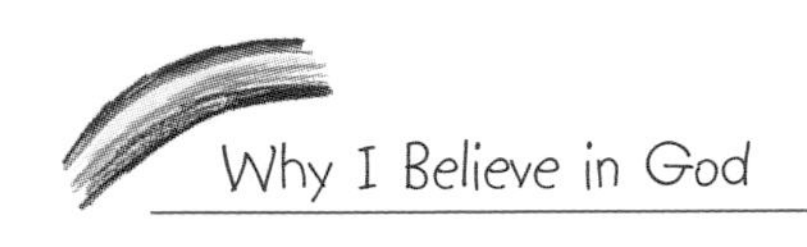

I Feel closest to God When I PRay. You can PRAY When You're laying down. And You can EVEN PRay When You're Standing on You'RE hed.

Taylor Ledon
AGE 6

Hi God!

God looks like a regular person, except cuter.

Kyle Scott Adkison
age 6

I believe that God is right next to me. I always leave a Spot in church for him

Jimmy Welsh
age 9

God knows alot of stuff that absolutely no one else in the world knows, such as how many hairs are on your head. But for people like my friend's grandfather, that question is easy because he has none.

Aubrie Beysselance
age 11

One reason I believe in God is that me and Mom and Dad were sleepy one day and the dog got out the gate. We prayed and we found the dog and it was a miracle just like the lost sheep.

Nicole Sheffield
age 6

My sister says you were born naked and you die naked, but I don't believe her.

Adam and Eve were naked but God helped them get clothes, and they started the whole clothes business.

Cody Hutchinson
age 7

God holds the whole world in his hands, and about everybody knows that. But he also holds Pluto and the sun and everything else, too, and people forget that.

Brent Glover
Age 8

When I get to heaven, I can sit and talk to God. I'll thank him first. It's always good to do more thanking than asking, It's one of the problems I have down here.

Paul Schoenfelder
age 7

God doesn't answer your prayers right after you asked. It takes awhile. Just like medicine. When you take it, it doesn't relieve you right away, it takes awhile for it to get in that place and dissolve in it. I don't know why He doesn't answer them right away. Trust me if I knew, I would tell everyone.

Hannah Welch
age 11

Everybody in the whole World sins,
So it's hard to get to heaven.
Nobody's whole body goes to heaven
So it's alot easier to travel
and for the angels to make
Pick-ups.

Scott Miles
age 7

God is the King of kings, and that means that all the earth kings, which includes the pres-idents, are not so big as they think they are.
And God is watching them too.

Nathan Troester
age 8

God makes us head-
first and then He
adds body and legs.
And last He reaches
inside his own
body and puts some
soul in us. And
He gives us guts.
His guts.

Jack Finlay
age 6

God makes the sunset just like a rainbow only he uses different color clouds and stirs them together so the colors are mixed. God makes us different colors too. It would get pretty old with all white people and nothing else.

Joshua LaBouliere
age 5

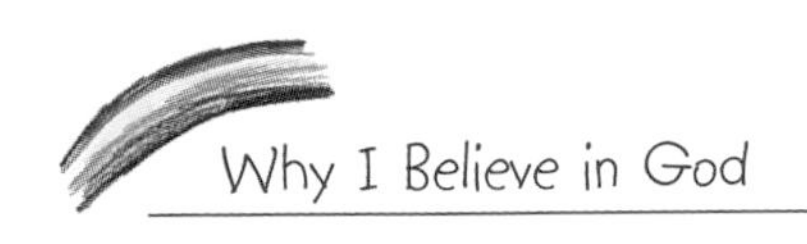

God can make me laugh.
I can make him laugh to,
but He has a lot on his
mind sometimes and it
doesn't work.

Shelby Hamilton
Age 7

I do not know exactly what the Lord looks like but I have an idea. I think he has brown hair and very pretty blue eyes. He probably has to do a lot of laundry because He wears white robes every day.

Nikki Greene
age 10

God's love feels like hot cocoa when you come inside from getting pushed in the snow.

Samantha Jann
age 9

God likes us to pray at meals. We bless the food becuase it gets stale otherwise. Night is a good time to pray too because you can say your sorry for the whole day.

Chelsea Decell
age 7

God is in love with your heart. He made people with hearts and people are harder to make than trees.

Sara Clogston
age 6

If I didn't believe in God, I wouldn't have any friends because I wouldn't be this nice.

Kelsi Wilson
age 6

God made everything just by saying it, but that doesn't mean he doesn't have to work hard. Some of the stuff he makes has to be done over and over again. Like light. God has to do light at least once a week.

Duncan MacDougall
age 6

God does not judge us by the way we look. God judges us by our heart and soul. I'm so happy God doesn't judge us by our looks 'cause I'd be a goner

Aimee Anderson
age 12

I know there's a God
because construction
people couldn't make
a planet.

Lindsey Hanner
age 9

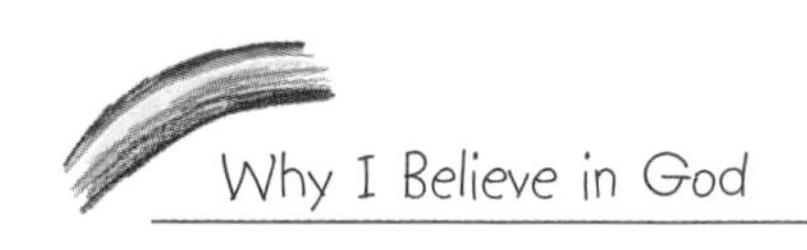

God made shoes so your socks won't get dirty. He makes laces so shoes won't fall off. And you get skin so your bones don't foll out.

Jack Finlay
age 6

When I die I think heaven will be bright and I will walk on streets of gold. God will be sitting on a gold throne reading the newspaper and drinking coffee. There will be angels and famous people like Julius Cesar, Jim Thorp, Roger williams, Aberham Lincoln

Scotty Oman
age 10

Kids know that candy is not better than God because candy can't love us. Plus God doesn't give you no cavities

Shelby Mack

age 7

DENTIST

Houses don't make it to heaven. TVs don't either. You don't bury a TV in the ground, So it can't go up. But that will be okay. There's Other Stuff to do in heaven.

Ashley Roth

age 5

God makes us babies so that we fit in our mother's stomach And he puts food in there that only babies like.

Brent Glover, age 8

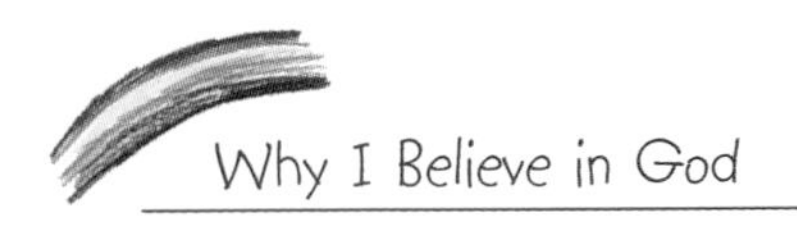

I'll tell You What God's love feels like—it feels like God is hugging you with his fur coat on.

Annie Siess
age 5

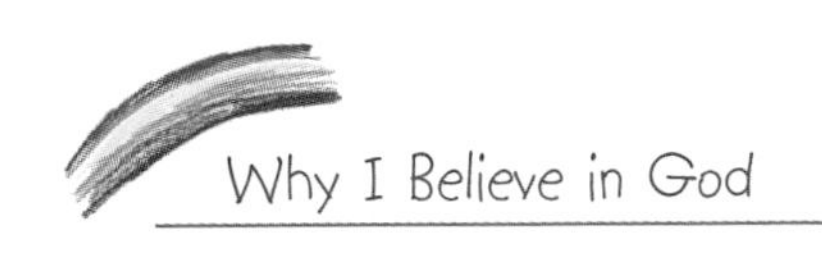

If I could give other kids advice, I'd give two advices. Freinds don't always know what's good for you but God does. And kids should never smoke at the bus stop - and neither should moms.

Meagan Bailey
age 7

In heaven, you do not have to make your bed. But you can if you want to. You never have to blow your nose because you do not have one. And heaven dose not have salad.

—Matthew Linakis—
age 8

God answers prayers but sometimes it takes time. He let my brother get chicken pox. We prayed he'd get better and he got better but it took alot of time and itching.

Craig Driskell
age 7

God gets sad if you tell a lie, if you hurt somebody, or if you sneeze on someone on purpose.

Shelby Hamilton
Age 7

It's like God is the garbage man (no offence) and our sins are the garbage. He'll take our sins and toss them in the garbage dump.

Lindsay Smith
age 9

some things that HAPPEN ARE HARd to UNDERSTAND LIKE WHY GOd MADE ROtWiLERS.

BRANCE BESS
age 5

I don't know if I hear God down here or not. Sometimes I think I hear my dad's voice, but it might be God. And other times I hear these bumps on the wall and I can't figure out the code if it's coming from God—it could just be bumps.

Kaleb Wood Ward
age 7

God is like a shepherd.
He watches over
us and makes sure we
don't walk off the edge.

Emily Landis
age 9

After everybody is done being nice and good on earth, we die. But before then, you may get to be something when you grown up, like a ballerina who takes care of horses.

Kelsey Mikkelson
age 6

If you believe in God, you will be sent to a place where everything goes right for you. There's no bloody bandaids, bad hair days, no days when you put a quarter in a machine and it takes your quarter. Nope, no days like that.

Jake Kendrick
age 11

God knows everything that you are thinking. But you should talk to Him anyway.

Madison Gregory
Age 10

So then MOM said.....
Rufff
ARF
Rufff ARF

God created dogs so that they
could listen patiently to children
when everyone else is busy.

Emilie Throop
age 11

God is the boss of the world

Sandy Lowry
age 9

I talk to God at supper, lunch, and night...and sometimes breakfast. He only talks back at night.

Kaitlin Nichol Wagner
age 7

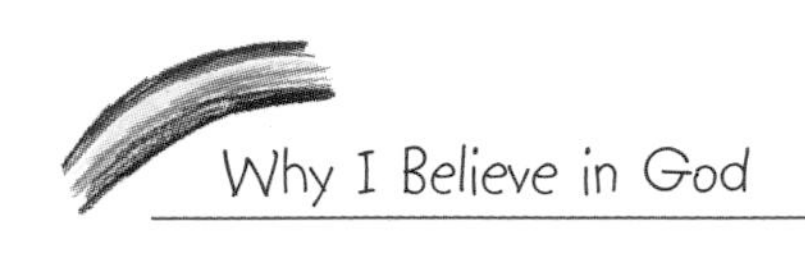

I can sing to God.
He likes the
God songs.

Kortney Fortier
age 7.

If you're good, God uses hiz God powers to call off gravity and zoom you to heaven. You might get wings and be an angel. That's what I want so I can go to heaven and meet my Papa.

Dakota Dispensire
5

People should remember that God made all of the minerals in the ground and not just gold so don't just get excited about gold. We need all the minerals.

Nathan Troester
age 8

WAW
WAW

Once I prayed for a brother or a sister for three years! I did not get a quick answer. He had to think about it first.

Bayli Whitterberg
age 9

God helps us with home work. How he does this is if it's hard, God gives you a brother and a sister to help. Maybe Dad and Mom if it's harder.

Robert Days
age 7

God tells us not to fight with our brothers and sisters because he Doesn't want anyone to get hurt. Cain and Mabel didn't listen to God and somebody did get hurt.

Sydney Walton
Age 5

I think God is real because no one can make a book that long he would be dead.

Corey Ommundsen
age 9

Holey
Bible

God looks down at us from
heaven and watches us when
we live in the city. We look kind
of like Hot Wheels tracks to
him.

Cullen Root
age 8

God has many jobs to do—like taking care Of the sun and helping trees grow. And he has three people working for him, but I can't remember their names.

Christian Andrew Gore, age 7

God makes everything
in the world. He makes
wood from his Skin and
rain from his tears
and I forget where
He gets Snow.

Timothy Gladney
age 8

God is my friend because when I don't have anyone to talk or play with, he is there for me, and I can talk to Him as much as I want and He won't even get bored of me talking even though I do talk a little bit too much sometimes.

Katie Dees
age 11

If I didn't believe in God life would be diffrent for me. For one thing I wouldn't get my work done. And for another thing I'd always have my name on the board.

Chelsea Decell
age 7

If you're not doing well in school pray. And try your best. God won't always help you if you don't try your best. He gets tired of that and has to answer another prayer. But he'll get back to you.

Dustin Laumbach
age 6

Amy, wake up dear.
I am praying!
Oh, sorry

It's Sad but
hobudy can
make people like
God.

Micah Ledon
age 7

I wonder if God sees me when i'm sleeping. But i'm asleep, so I can't know that part.

Linnea Totushek

Age 6

No Dirt
IN
HEAVEN

I think heaven is the best thing in the universe. Heaven has hills where instead of getting dirty you get clean when you roll down.

Andy Clegg, age 9

God gives me a sister to love and it helps me learn to be nice. Sometimes my brother is mean to me. I say, I love you. And he says it back, then says he's just Kidding. But if you can get along with your brother and sister, you can get along with anyone.

Kelsi Wilson
age 6

Sometimes when I`m unhappy, God tickles me.

Beaux Martin
age 5

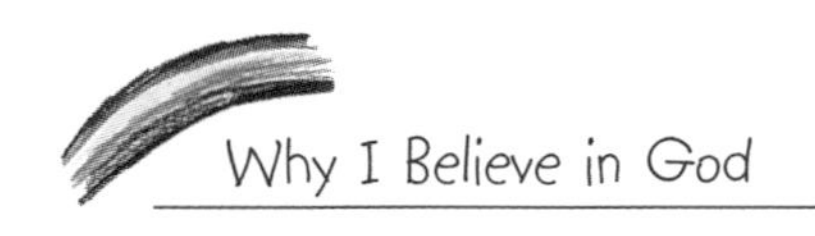

A very good thing about God is that he fits in your heart.

Sarah Gendron
Age 5

Acknowledgments

Thanks so much to all the children who took time and energy to share their thoughts and artwork on God. I learned from all of you! Special thanks go to:

Schools

Ashland Christian School and Grace Brethren Church –
Ashland, OH
Barrington Christian Academy –
Barrington, RI
Blue Ridge Christian School –
Kansas City, MO
Calvsa Preparatory School –
Miami, FL
Commmunity Christian Schools –
Norman, OK
Divine Savior School –
Norridge, IL
Donelson Christian Academy –
Nashville, TN
First Covenant Church –
Sacramento, CA
Margaret Garrison, Director of Children's Ministries
First Lutheran School –
Torrance, CA
Grace Academy for Christian Discipleship –
York, PA
Highview Baptist School –
Louisville, KY
Holy Cross School –
West Sacramento, CA
Julie M. Brehl
Marcia Cornelius
Mary Our Queen Catholic Grade School –
Omaha, NE
Monteverde Friends School –
Costa Rica, CA
Nampa Christian School –
Nampa, ID
Neuman School –
Mansfield, OH
Oklahoma Christian Schools –
Edmond, OK
Parkview Baptist School –
Baton Rouge, LA
Sacred Heart Academy –
San Diego, CA
Snohomish County Christian School –
Lynnwood, WA
St. Clement School –
Westlake, OH
St. Edwards School of Ashland, Trinity Lutheran Church –
Ashland, OH
St. Francis School –
Warrick, RI
St. John's Christian School –
Roseville, CA
St. Joseph School –
Sacramento, CA
Marsha Cornelius
St. Mary School
St. Therese School –
Garfield, OH
St. William School –
Chicago, IL
Tabernacle School –
Concord, CA
Linda Richardson

Acknowledgments

Individuals

Ashley Aguirre
Shelby Akre
Megan Archuleta
Tessa Azevedo
Ariana Barrios
Skylar Betancourt
Stephon Birdwell
Kristen Borde
Delilah Brookins
Enrique Campos
John Campos
Jacob Coates
Willie Conkling
Ximmer Conkling
Darien Countrymen
Annie Cowan
Grace Cowan
Joey Cowan
Wesley Daniels
Katy Davis
Stuart Davis
Anne de Guzman
Nai-muh Dennis
Thomas DesRosier
Tiara Diaz
Alexander Dominitz
Andrew Dominitz
Joe Donner
Sara Dunlop
Norris Eldridge
Samantha Essman
Risa Farrell
Sara Farrell
Anthony Garfio
Marissa Garner
Kevin-John Greenlese
Kimber Greenlese
Ariel Gregersen
Lanessa Guerra
Julian Gutierrez
Christopher Hall
Haley Homan
Spencer Jenkins
Brandon Lamb
Carissa Larsen
Sarah Lehua Sanarez
Elia Lonestar
Alyssa Lopez
Adam MacDonald
Janae Mayfield
Kimberly McCormack
Sarrah McCormack
Lois McEndree
Reggie Meigs
Daniel Mendoza
Cody Mertz
Rebecca Mertz
Tyler Mertz
Ryan Miles
Alex Miller
Ian Miller
Kelly Miller
Josh Mitchell
Vanessa Murillo
Victoria Naungayan
Andrea Navarrete
Melissa O'Brien
Dusty O'Connor
Jacquelyn Paré
Roger Pastrana
Matthew Pereira
Madison Pierce
Drew Poland
Stephanie Poland
Nick Pruglo
Edgar Ramirez
Oscar Ramov
Kristy Read
Nina Reyes
Diane Rodriguez
Jessica Rome
Kyle San Clemente
MaileRae Sanarez
Kevin Schwieger
Scott Schwieger
Michael Scribner
Alison Seamons
Marley Smith
Tara Tessmann
Mallory Trojan
Melissa Urian
Tammy Urian
Angelina Valdez
Katie Walton
Peter Walton
Sydney Walton
LeAlta Wells
Leilani Wells
Sydney Werry
Ashley Wibberley
Shatashia Williams
David Wilson